LET'S VISIT...

ENGLAND

Annabelle Lynch

W
FRANKLIN WATTS

Franklin Watts
Published in Great Britain in 2016
by The Watts Publishing Group

Editor: Julia Bird
Designer: Jeni Child

Dewey classification number: 942
PB ISBN 978 1 4451 3700 1

Printed in China

Photo acknowledgements:
Adelie Penguin/Dreamstime: 6r. I Aksoy/
Shutterstock: 5t. Anizza/Dreamstime: 1, 17t.
Atg images/Dreamstime: 9t. Martin Beddall/
Alamy: 12c. Dan Breckwort/Dreamstime:
14c. Ashley Cooper/Alamy: 12b. Roger
Coulam/Alamy: 9c. Howard Davies/Alamy:
front cover, 18b. Viorel Dudau/Dreamstime:
16c. Christopher Elwell/Dreamstime: 4-5.
Gregg Balfour Evans/Alamy: 19t, 19b.
Markus Gann/Dreamstime: 10-11. Jeff
Greenberg/Alamy: 9b. Russell Hart/Alamy:
15t. John Hill 118/Dreamstime: 4b. David
Hughes/Dreamstime: 13t. Jaroslaw Killan/
Dreamstime: 18c. Anastasiia Kucherenko/
Shutterstock: 4tl, 6tl, 6bl, 8tl, 10tl, 12tl, 14tl,
16tl, 18tl, 20tl. Paul Maguire/Dreamstime:
10bl. Doug McKinley/Getty Images: 21t.
Derrick Neill/Dreamstime: 3bl, 7br. Pajda
83/Dreamstime: 2, 11t. Cornelia Paladuta/
Dreamstime: 17bl, 17bt. Purple Marbles
York 1/Alamy: 21b. Daniel Rushall/Alamy:
11b. Darren Turner/Dreamstime: 3br, 8b.
Wikipedia: 15b. Kenny Williamson/Alamy: 7tl.
Anna Yakimova/Dreamstime: 20c.

Franklin Watts
An imprint of
Hachette Children's Group
Part of The Watts Publishing Group
Carmelite House
50 Victoria Embankment
London EC4Y 0DZ

An Hachette UK Company
www.hachette.co.uk
www.franklinwatts.co.uk

CONTENTS

Let's Visit England 4

The Lake District 6

Alnwick Castle 8

The Jurassic Coast 10

The National Space Centre 12

St Ives 14

The Natural History Museum 16

Legoland 18

Jorvik Viking Centre 20

Map of England 21

Glossary 22

Index and Further Information..........24

Words in **bold** are in the glossary.

LET'S VISIT
ENGLAND

England is the biggest country in the United Kingdom (UK). It stretches from Scotland in the north to Wales in the west. The rest of England is surrounded by sea.

What does it look like?

England's countryside is mostly green and flat, with some rolling hills. In the north, the **landscape** is more rugged, with some higher hills and mountains. England has a long coastline, with lots of long beaches and high, rocky cliffs.

 A sandy beach at the seaside town of Skegness, in north-east England.

Around 70 per cent of England's countryside is used for farming.

 The famous Tower Bridge is found in London. It crosses the River Thames.

In the city

England's biggest city is its **capital**, London. It is found in the south-east corner of England. Other big cities include Birmingham, Manchester and Liverpool.

TRAVEL TIP

If you visit London, try a boat cruise down the Thames. It's a great way to see the city.

When to go

England's weather changes all the time! The sunny spring and summer months are usually the best time to visit, although it can still rain.

THE LAKE DISTRICT

The wild, beautiful Lake District is found in the north-west of England. It is a very popular area to visit and welcomes millions of tourists every year.

 ## Protected place

The landscape of the Lake District is very dramatic, with high mountains and deep, blue lakes. The Lake District is a national park, which means that the land is protected and any new building work is carefully planned.

 ### TRAVEL TIP

If you go walking, remember to follow the countryside code. Follow the path, pay attention to any **signs**, don't disturb any plants or animals and take any litter home with you.

Things to do

The Lake District is a wonderful place to explore the great outdoors. You can walk, cycle or take a boat ride around the lakes, try your luck at fishing or take in the views from England's highest mountains. You can even have a go at the Treetop Trek, with its wobbly rope bridges, slides and thrilling 250-metre zip wire ride.

⬆ **Fly through the air on the Treetop Trek** zip wire!

OTHER GREAT
NATIONAL PARKS:
The Peak District
The New Forest
The South Downs

Rainy days

If it rains (and it often does!), there is still plenty to do. You can visit the dinosaurs at the Keswick Dinosaur and Raptor Experience, go climbing at the indoor climbing centre at Kendal or take a ride on a lakeside steam train.

⬆ **The Lakeside and Haverthwaite railway** runs for 5 kilometres between Haverthwaite and Lake Windermere.

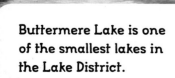

Buttermere Lake is one of the smallest lakes in the Lake District. ⬆

ALNWICK CASTLE

Alnwick Castle is one of the most famous and spectacular castles in northern England. If it looks familiar, you might have seen it in the *Harry Potter* films!

Fortress Alnwick

There has been a castle at Alnwick for over a thousand years. It is the home of the Duke of Northumberland and was first built to defend the English border against **invaders** from Scotland. Over the years, it has seen plenty of fierce battles.

TRAVEL TIP

When you buy a ticket for the castle, you can visit it again for free for a whole year.

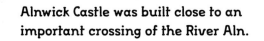
Alnwick Castle was built close to an important crossing of the River Aln.

See for yourself

Today, the castle is open to everyone. You can explore the grand state rooms where dukes of the past lived, browse through the 14,000 books in the library or tiptoe into the spooky Lost Cellars. Outside, you can visit the gruesome Poison Garden or explore the huge Alnwick Treehouse.

 The Alnwick Treehouse is one of the biggest treehouses in the world.

 A guide on the *Harry Potter* tour, complete with a barn owl.

Take part

There is a lot to do at Alnwick Castle. You can dress up in **medieval** clothes, try **archery** or take part in a **falcon** show. *Harry Potter* fans should see the Battleaxe to Broomsticks Tour and take part in a broomstick flying lesson!

 Try dressing up as a knight. Don't forget your trusty horse!

THREE **CASTLES** TO SEE:

Warwick Castle
Corfe Castle
Windsor Castle

9

THE JURASSIC COAST

The spectacular Jurassic coast stretches for over 150 kilometres along the south-west coast of England. It was England's first **World Heritage Site.**

Fabulous fossils

The Jurassic coast is especially famous for its rocks. These rocks tell the story of how the island of Britain formed millions of years ago. Many important **fossils** have been found here over the years, from fish and plants to giant **reptiles** and even dinosaurs!

TRAVEL TIP

Charmouth beach is one of the best places for fossil hunters. You can even go on a special fossil-hunting tour.

 Fossils show us what animals looked like millions of years ago. This is the fossil of a fish.

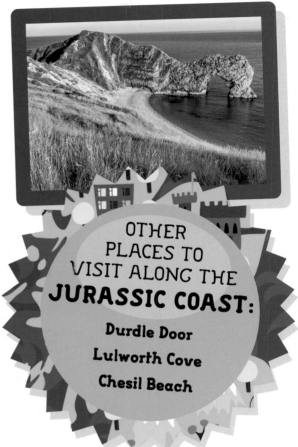

Durdle Door's soft rock has been shaped over millions of years.

OTHER PLACES TO VISIT ALONG THE **JURASSIC COAST:**

Durdle Door

Lulworth Cove

Chesil Beach

Go on a fossil hunt

You can collect fossils for yourself at most places along the Jurassic coast. All you need is sturdy shoes for scrambling over rocks and a bag to put your fossils in. The best places to look are among the pebbles and rockpools on the shore – you can often find fossils of creatures called ammonites here.

Have fun, but take care, when you're looking for fossils. Stay away from cliffs, where rocks can fall.

THE NATIONAL SPACE CENTRE

See stars at the National Space Centre! It is found in Leicester, in the heart of England.

Astronaut for the day

The National Space Centre is the best place in England to find out all about the wonders of space and space travel. As well as over 150 hand-on challenges to tackle, you can explore a real Russian **spacecraft**, see the space suit that was worn by Laika, the first dog in space, and even attempt to land a rocket on the Moon in the Spaceflight Induction Module.

Soyuz spacecraft have been used for space travel since the 1960s.

 ## Movie time

If all that has tired you out, you can watch a show in the UK's biggest **planetarium**. These amazing 360° films take you on a journey through the **solar system** and show you the stars of the night sky.

⬆ The National Space Centre looks out over the River Soar.

 ### TRAVEL TIP

Check before you go, but the Space Centre often hosts special events. Real-life astronauts often come here to talk about life in space, and in 2014, some of the Star Wars actors appeared here.

OTHER **FUN PLACES** TO VISIT NEARBY:

Bradgate Country Park

Snibston Museum and Country Park

Great Central Railway

13

ST IVES

The town and harbour of St Ives.

If you like going to the seaside, St Ives is one of the best places to visit in England.

Golden sands

The seaside town and **port** of St Ives is found in Cornwall, on the very south-west edge of England. Its fine, sandy beach (Porthmeor) stretches for a kilometre along the Atlantic coast.

Surf's up! One of St Ives' surfing schools gets ready to tackle the waves.

TRAVEL TIP

One of the best ways to arrive in St Ives is on the local train. It winds its way along the coast and has great views of the sea and cliffs.

Water fun

Porthmeor beach is a great place to go to try out all sorts of water sports. You can learn to surf, sea kayak or even have a go on a stand-up paddleboard with the local surf school. Or if you prefer, you can just have a paddle in the sea or build a huge sandcastle!

Other things to do

The town of St Ives has always attracted artists, who love to paint St Ives' beautiful sea views. Today, you can visit the famous Tate St Ives where lots of paintings of the area are kept. You can also take part in an activity trail all around the gallery and its gardens.

OTHER GREAT PLACES TO VISIT
IN CORNWALL:
The Cornish Seal Sanctuary
St Michael's Mount
The Eden Project

Tate St Ives has lots of fun, creative activities to take part in, especially during school holidays.

15

THE NATURAL HISTORY MUSEUM

Are you interested in finding out about the world around us? Then the Natural History Museum in London is the place for you.

Get up close with a dinosaur at the Natural History Museum.

Earth zones

The Natural History Museum is in four zones. The blue zone looks at animals, from tiny insects to huge dinosaurs. The green zone explores plants, while the red zone is all about Planet Earth. The orange zone takes in the wildlife gardens and the Darwin Centre, where you can learn how we are protecting the natural world.

TRAVEL TIP

In summer, the museum hosts a butterfly house in its wildlife garden. In winter, there is an ice-skating rink.

Skate the night away at the winter ice-skating rink.

 # Best bits

There is so much to see at the Natural History Museum that you might get a bit tired! Here are some things that you won't want to miss: the life-size model of a huge blue whale, the **skeleton** of a giant 26-metre-long dinosaur called a diplodocus and the **earthquake** room where you can feel the ground shiver and shake, just like in a real earthquake.

OTHER **MUSEUMS** TO VISIT:

The British Museum

The Science Museum

The Horniman Museum

An escalator leads up to the museum's red zone.

Make sure you see the model of a blue whale – the biggest mammal on Earth.

LEGOLAND

Legoland in Windsor is a **theme park** where it is all about Lego! It welcomes two million visitors a year.

Model magic

Legoland is most famous for its Lego models. In Miniland you can walk through mini towns and cities made entirely of Lego. Other Lego models are dotted around the park, including famous people, animals and even the **cockpit** of an aeroplane.

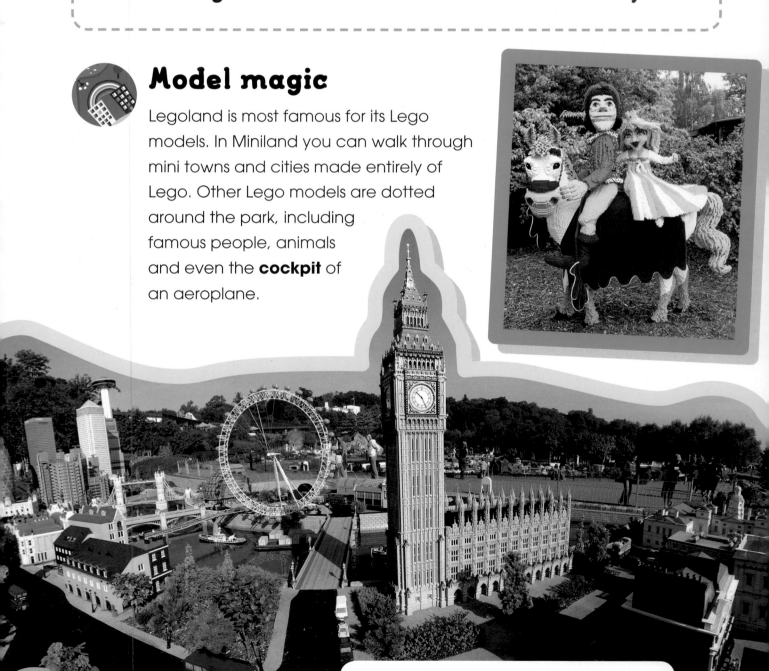

Visit Miniland to see the London sights, including Big Ben and London buses.

 Get a soaking in Legoland's duplo water park.

Discover and do

There are lots of workshops in Legoland where you can make and test your very own big models with a bit of help from the people who work there. There are also lots of exciting rides to try, from cars to rollercoasters and from boats to amazing **submarines**. There is even a big, splashy water park with slides, fountains and big toys – so don't forget to bring your swimsuit!

 TRAVEL TIP

If you don't like queuing for the rides (and who does?) you can rent a Q-bot. This lets you reserve a go on a ride at a certain time. You have to pay for it though!

Have fun at the driving school, but watch out for the traffic lights!

SOME OTHER **GREAT THEME** PARKS TO TRY:
Chessington World of Adventures
Alton Towers
Diggerland

JORVIK VIKING CENTRE

Meet the Vikings at the Jorvik Viking Centre! It is found in York, in the north of England.

Who were the Vikings?

The Vikings were brave, fierce sailors who invaded Britain over a thousand years ago. They settled in parts of England, including York, and started a new life there.

The Vikings arrived in Britain in longships, looking for new lands.

Dig and find

Between 1976 and 1981 **archaeologists** worked at a site in York. They found the remains of a Viking town: buildings, workshops, backyards and toilets, as well as thousands of pots and other crafts. These helped them to understand how the Vikings lived.

SOME OTHER **GREAT PLACES** TO VISIT IN YORK:

National Railway Museum

The York Dungeon

York Minster

An actor shows off a traditional Viking battle helmet at the Jorvik Centre. →

See for yourself

At the Jorvik Viking Centre, the world of the Vikings has been carefully recreated. You can sit by the fireside in a Viking home, go shopping in a busy market place, watch craftsmen at work in a workshop or even visit a Viking pigsty! Viking sounds and smells help to make you feel as though you are really stepping back in time.

TRAVEL TIP

Every year, there is a Jorvik Viking Festival in York where people dress up as Vikings. You can watch battles and competitions, including the strongest Viking and best beard competitions!

MAP OF ENGLAND

KEY:
- 1 The Lake District
- 2 Alnwick Castle
- 3 The Jurassic Coast
- 4 The National Space Centre
- 5 St Ives
- 6 The Natural History Museum
- 7 Legoland
- 8 Jorvik Viking Centre

GLOSSARY

archaeologist
Someone who digs up objects to find out about the past

archery
The sport of shooting at a target with a bow and arrow

capital
The city where a country's government meets

cockpit
The place in an aeroplane where the pilot sits

earthquake
When the ground shakes violently

falcon
A bird of prey

fossil
The traces in rock of animals or plants that lived millions of years ago

invaders
People who enter another country by force

landscape
Everything you can see when you look at an area, such as hills, forests, rivers and buildings

longship
A long, narrow boat with oars

mammal
A creature with hair that gives birth to babies and feeds them on its milk

medieval
From a period of history called the Middle Ages. This lasted from around the 5th to the 15th centuries CE

planetarium
A big room in which the planets and stars are shown on a rounded ceiling

port
A place by the sea from where boats and ships arrive and depart

reptile
A cold-blooded animal with scales, such as a crocodile

sign
A poster or board which gives you information or a warning. A road sign, for example, tells you about how fast you can go on a road

skeleton
All the bones in a body joined together

solar system
The Sun and all the planets that go around it, including Earth

spacecraft
A rocket or vehicle that can travel in space

submarine
A boat that can travel underwater

theme park
A large park with rides such as rollercoasters

World Heritage Site
A place or building that is particularly special or important and is protected by law

zip wire
A rope or cable stretched between two places that you can slide down attached to a harness

INDEX

Alnwick Castle 8–9, 22

beaches 4, 10–11, 14–15

castles 8–9
Cornwall 14–15

Durdle Door 11

farming 4
fossils 10–11

Harry Potter 8–9

Jorvik Viking Centre 20–22
Jurassic coast 10–11, 22

Lake District 6–7, 22
landscape 4, 6–9
Legoland 18–19, 22
Leicester 12–13
London 5, 16–18

map 22
mountains 4, 6–7

museums 13, 16–17, 20–22

national parks 6–7
National Space Centre 12–13, 22
Natural History Museum 16–17, 22

St Ives 14–15, 22

weather 5, 7

York 20–21

FURTHER INFORMATION

Books

Fact Cat: England by Alice Harman (Wayland, 2014)

Living in the UK: England by Annabelle Lynch (Franklin Watts, 2014)

Websites

www.visitengland.com

www.treetoptrek.co.uk

www.spacecentre.co.uk